THE
ANCHOR
OF
REALITY

Annie Hope

Metamorphosis
Creative Productions
— LLC —

This book is dedicated to all those suffering from the disease of addiction, whether directly or through the pain carried by those who love them.

And to Harry Dixon Loes, whose timeless song *This Little Light of Mine* has echoed in my heart for years, reminding me to let my light shine—no matter what.

Let it shine, let it shine, let it shine.

How This Began

Loving an addict will make you feel insane. The emotions don't just conflict—they contradict. Hope and grief in the same breath. Rage and tenderness for the same person. I turned to writing and drawing to survive it. What began as survival slowly became a refuge.

Over the years—through relapses, betrayals, and broken promises—poems emerged. Sketches followed. Sometimes the drawings came first. Sometimes the poems did. Together, they began to tell a story I hadn't yet learned how to say out loud.

This book chronicles my journey from losing control of my life to surrendering what I could not change—my partner's addiction—and, in doing so, finding a quieter kind of peace. Not resolution. Not closure. But acceptance—of his path, and eventually, my own.

Some of these poems were written on the worst days of my life. Others came after the dust settled, when I could finally see what the chaos had taken from me—my presence, my sense of self, the years I spent consumed with trying to keep someone alive, keep him sober, save our love. I had become a shell of a person. The work itself became a way back to my own voice, my boundaries, my worth.

If you are struggling with addiction, or loving someone who is, I may not know you personally—but I understand. I know the relentless thoughts. The pit in your stomach every morning, knowing your life is falling apart while you smile and say everything is fine. The loneliness of lying to protect him—because if people knew, they'd ask why you were still there. And how do you explain that you stayed because you loved him? Because you believed you could save him?

Showing up anyway. That takes strength most people will never understand.

I'm not here to promise you healing. But I made it to the other side
— and for a long time I never thought I would. I never wanted to
leave. I imagined a happy ending for us right up until I couldn't
anymore. If you have ever loved an addict, these pages are for you.
If I can find my way out of something I never wanted to escape,
maybe this can at least show you that it's possible. You are not as
alone as you feel. And you are not as crazy as you think.

Contents

Section IV: The Turning

Section V: The Becoming

Before You Begin

Dear Reader,

I didn't write this all at once.
I wrote it from the middle,
from the edge,
from the breaking,
and finally,
from the breath that came after.

Some of these poems are soft-spoken cries.
Some are love letters I never sent.
Some are goodbyes I had to write twice—
three times,
more times than I can count.

You might meet a version of me
who waited too long,
who begged,
who still believed.
That version of me wasn't weak.
She was just still holding on
to the dream
that love could fix what it didn't cause.

If you see yourself in her—
know that I do too.

And know this:
the letting go didn't happen in one day.
But I began.
You can, too.

With care,
Annie Hope

Section I: The Shattering

This is where the breaking begins—
where love hurts more than it heals,
and truth whispers through the cracks.

The Anchor of Reality pt. 1

'A weight on my shoulders' may be a cliché,
but it's my entire being.

I drown
in my lover's demons,
to keep him afloat.

A knowing crept through me,
subtle then,
cold splash on my toes,
dark liquid reaching for me.

A faint suppressed help
escapes your lips.

You're drowning; tumultuous waters.
I have every intention to save you,
believing
I can rescue you without harm.

Ignoring intuition, I push
forward, uncomfortable.

Against my will.
That's what we do for love.

Submerged, I feel my ankle shackled
to yours; chains clink, your addiction
sinks me.

I ache for sunlight's touch,
for breath that rises with ease,
the calm
as grass bows to breeze.

I gaze at soulless eyes,
a reverse thousand yard stare,
an unrecognizable face
I knew so well once.

You point to your chains,
promise if I help, you'll swim
for both of us;
I do,
sacrificing me for you.

Gasping for air.
I look up and see you afloat—
it is my submerged
body—that keeps you
buoyant.

I am the anchor of reality.

Sinking
with your demons,
your insecurities,
heavy-hearted.

Frantic,
each beat visibly thudding.

I swam into these treacherous waters
so easily and called it love.

The cinder blocks hit rock bottom,
pressure ripples fiercely,
through the eerie, silent water.

My body, in a white nightgown,
submerged.

I am pale as porcelain—with swollen,
water-filled lungs.

Golden hair sways
with the water's rhythm,
eyes that glimpse
the flickering surface,
the man I love,
hoping he notices
that he is drowning me.

KNOCK KNOCK

Knock. Knock.
An ordinary night, I made tea.
You were quiet,
staring through the steam,
and then we heard it—

Knock.
Knock.
You answered the door.

On our doorstep it stood,
uninvited, unnamed.
You didn't flinch.
You welcomed it
like an old friend.

I watched you offer it a seat,
pour a drink,
laugh too hard.
I waited for you to come to bed,
but the sheets were never touched.

You called it comfort.
I called it a death sentence.

Something shifted.
Silence roared.
The way light left your eyes.
The way the stranger—

switched places with me.

The uninvited guest,
that shattered our life.
It didn't ask for permission.
You didn't ask for mine.
You let it in,
handed it the key.

Holding On

I walk through a forest, willows upon willows,
dreams spun from silk, stitched into my pillows.
Which branch will I pick?
Which one will I choose?
My greatest support.
My crutch.
My muse.

I thought I could choose the perfect one—
a branch kissed by sun, my fairytale spun.
The air was soft, the willows kind,
I chased the plan—etched
like pages in a storybook,
deep in my mind.

A branch above—strong,
serene—
held all the love
I'd ever dare dream.

Then a thunderstorm hit,
the sky split.
You reached for comfort elsewhere,
and in that shift,
you changed your course.

Every day you're here,
you're really not.
If your snap
is inevitable—
it must be preventable.

But the bark splinters,
my hands now bleed.
It was never going to be
without resistance.

And now
I resist you.

I hold and hold,
the days peeling away.

Go.
I want you still—
stay, even as I tear.

You're my only branch... or so I believe,
the story never said
I'd have to leave.

The fairytale fades,
like breath on glass.
I stare at my reflection,
unsure who I'll be
if I stay.

Once a dream,
now turning nightmare—
must I fall
to save the story
I was trying to live?

Thread

Stitch me up, don't vanish
into your haze.

I cry out for help,
but you glance and walk away.

The small gash
widened silently.

I needed more than care,
I needed you—
your touch
to heal me.

Briefly.

To staunch the
cut—
you pressed
deeper.

What remains of care,
when love stays but
the hands don't.

And yet—
you rage
behind your gaze.

Through the haze—
tend to me—

You glance
away,
indifferent.

You watch the blood
swell.

You hear my screams
while I bleed out.

I see your veil.
I wear one too.

Am I the infection,
or the infected?

My hands in blood—
you,
already nowhere.

And still,
I wait.

And still,
I am alone.

To the Battle We Became

Oh, we fell so hard
in love, a gift (wasn't it?)
Us against the world,
until the world went quiet
around us.

What creature waits, sly
below the hardwood desk, climbing
into your mind, inside my watching eye
as you unravel.

Hearing its everything-promise,
how alive it makes you feel.
What vows it whispers, long-lashed
mellifluous sequences of words.

Maybe it gave you two hearts,
sugar-laced air, a silent mind,
stamina— for what? A dream,
something to fill every hour.

How gentle the trick
when fantasy weaves its veil
in silk syllables. Asking for a price
even though you offered it everything.

Another battle too good
not to fight, but don't you see?
The war is you vs you.
It takes utterly all and nothing
from me.

It takes
my sanity.

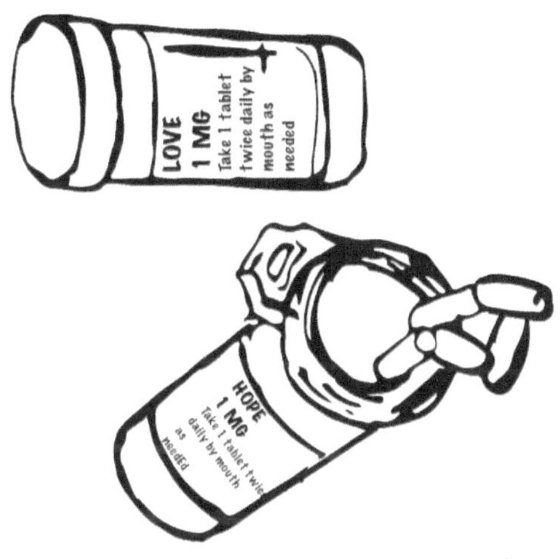

LOVE
1 MG
Take 1 tablet
twice daily by
mouth as
needed
HOPE
1 MG
Take 1 tablet twice
daily by mouth
as
needed

Painkiller

Like a surfer
chasing the high of a barrel,
disregarding the wipeout,
I'm caught in a cycle with no shore.

Relief arrives in waves,
easing the unknown.
All day, I crave
you—
my painkiller,
my validation.

I can't stand abandonment.
Life is a dagger,
always twisting.
How do I survive
losing while living?

You're sitting next to me,
a stranger in my soulmate's skin.
I suppress my feelings,
my inner compass,
neglected,
as I cling to your words.

I become the addict,
you have always been.

To numb the pain—

Hope,
my painkiller,
may kill me still.

Oblivion

Sleep lets me go.
Morning doesn't.

Sleep loosens its grip:
the room goes quiet,
for a moment
my heart lifts
before it falls.

Then it drops—
weight on my chest.
The ceiling.
Unmoved.

Pain floods back in,
heat under the skin—
whatever vanished at night
is waiting with the day.

Each dream becomes the life
I wake up fearing.
I want to stay where I'm unreachable,
where nothing can touch me.

I thought I could disappear there—
but my broken heart followed me in.

And still my eyes open—
I don't know why.
Sleep is the only place
the pain forgets my name.

Fever Dream

At night, I leave myself.
Sleep dulls the edges.
Love feels possible again—

as if once
the phone were filled with messages,
as if we knew what we were holding
or wanted it too much
to understand it.

Something too beautiful to survive.

A creature with no gills
learning to live at sea.
Quietly insane.
In love again.

Morning interrupts.

The screen is empty.
I dial your number halfway,
stop.
Dial again.

I rehearse a future anyway—
places that almost were:
passengers of our Star Train,
Westbound flights,
becoming creatures of the sand.

I don't call.
Every morning,
my heart drops
back onto its body.

Flatline

Yesterday,
you held me like this connection
was the reason I was here at all—
my head rising to the rhythm of your breath,
your chest hair brushing my nose,
your scent pulling me under,
your fingers drifting through my hair.
A warmth so convincing
I let my guard
unclench
for the first time in years.

And then—
hours slipped,
a minute cracked,
a second misfired—
and suddenly your eyes
forgot how to know me.
Your pupils
belonging to someone—
something else.

How does love evaporate
that fast?
How does a heart go from full
to desolate
in the space between
goodnight
and nothing?

Every pulse,
squeezed—
chambers collapsing,
blood draining,
valves splintering—
until even hope
coughed itself out on the floor.

Sick and Tired

I wake knowing what to expect.
It's always there.

I look for you without meaning to—
your initial on glass,
your face in every crowd.

Smiles fall flat.
None are yours.

The screen stays blank.
Even my hope stops refreshing.

Whatever was left
stopped blooming altogether.
  "I love you."
    "I love you not."

I feel cold
now that I've stopped begging.

Still, the pull—
a wave I can't outrun.

(I drift through conversations,
a shell where I should be.)

This ache feels permanent—
an extra beat
I never asked for.

And the worst of it:
I would still follow you anywhere
for the version of you
that disappeared.

Hope, Worn Through

It doesn't arrive suddenly—
gradual,
agonizing.

Initially,
she's resilient,
full of solutions,
armed with prayers.

But as the storm persists,
she realizes
this isn't her battle,
not her fight—
and she lets go.

The death begins—
deliberate—
taking everything with it.

Days string together,
weeks unravel,
a lingering demise—
until
hope dies.

Section II: The Spiral

What we can't let go, we relive.
Over and over.
Hoping for different endings
to the same story.

I ♥ YOU
love

Film of Memories

Memories unwind
like scenes from our greatest lie.
Rewriting lines, replaying scenes,
putting our love story on a loop—
montaging it
again.

Frame by frame—five seasons
sped up, projecting us into
another time.

We added the highlights and fades,
but only I wrote the credits,
in my tears.
I screamed them out,
knowing they'd never roll.

We only made a vision of our movie,
a movie of our vision.
The scenes stayed trapped
inside the script.

The soundtrack lingers,
a refrain echoing through corridors,
as the film of memories plays on.

Prey

I don't remember it.

It remembers me—

my heart
standing in the open.

A white lamb in a field,
not knowing
a wolf hides in the brush,

already chosen,
before it even knows how to run.

White-Knuckled Love

You're pacing by the window,
I'm holding back my scream.
You say you'll change tomorrow—
give you one more chance to dream.

Lifeboat (The Storm)

The bow dives into the wave,
the stern lifts, exposed.
Holes in the hull take on water,
the wind screams through torn sails.

Waves hammer the deck,
the mast creaks, hollow—
I brace for impact.

Before my captain sees the damage,
I sew the sail,
jury-rig the rudder,
call out to you:
we can survive the storm.

The waves return, crashing over the rails.
My hands bleed,
clutching the lines.
The boom swings—
a near death roll.
I throw my weight to starboard,
ease the tilt.
Still, I smile and whisper,
we can survive the storm.

At night, below deck,
I let the storm in.
My tears fall quietly
where no one can see.

My captain mustn't know
the ship is going under.
I would sacrifice everything
to keep it afloat.

Not for me—
for him.

As captain, you choose
to drown in your addiction.

And I am left
between the lifeboat
and sinking with you.

Bonfire

You just keep lighting yourself on fire,
puzzled by the burn,
circling your own
raging bonfire.

Sparks you ignite—
moments of warmth—
enough to reach for.

Hands reach in.
Clothes catch.

You throw on water.
Steam surges.

You smother the flames—
the fire spreads.

By the time you're dancing
with the flames, you don't know
what fed it, or what was trying to
save you.

Lifeboat (Forgotten)

You are the hero,
the captain,
the main character,
destined to live in your own movie.

You don't see
the lifeboat
through the storm
you chose.

The Merry-Go-Round

Around and around and around I go—
bright lights blur,
a horse rising and falling
to a waltz I didn't choose.

I laugh when it lifts me,
go quiet when it drops.
The music keeps time
better than I do.
Has it always sounded off-key?

I've memorized the chipped paint on the pole,
the false ending of the song—
the pause that feels like stopping,
before it starts again.

It looks like joy from the outside.

The crowd that once smiled
now watches in fear.

The pace quickens—
my hands
tighten on the pole,
knuckles white.

I look for an exit—
a signal, a lever,
a way off that doesn't feel like falling.

And for the first time,
I don't want to go on.
I just don't know
how to leave.

Dr. Jekyll & Mr. Hyde

I can't blame myself for falling in love.
I didn't see what stayed hidden.

Not long after,
Mr. Hyde surfaced.
Still,
I searched for you—
mistaking cycles for balance.

The damage should have been enough.
It wasn't.

I waited
for the man I knew
to find his way back.

I stayed.
I defended.
And somewhere along the way,
I became the enemy.

After each relapse,
you came back
wearing guilt like an open wound.

You promised again,
he wouldn't come back.

I took your hand,
already counting days—
knowing the one who returns
never stays.

No Contact

They say this is the way to heal—
but how do you grieve a ghost
still flickering
in your palms?

Our invisible string
cut,
the signal fades.
I stand in silence—
ringing in my ears.

Your contact erased,
but still carved in me.
Each digit, a shadow
I press with my mind,
trying not to remember.

Each day, I whisper release
through a throat of thorns.
This is the cure, they say—
but it burns like a prayer
I don't want to say.

Words Left Unspoken

Something in the way disease endures
traps me—
not for what it is,
but for how I can't stop thinking
about love,
or about enduring love
as much as enduring this disease.

> Relentless, isn't it? Seizing hearts,
> scarring your body,
> etching through me—
> not clean, not quick, but gouging.
> Again and again.
> And then, one day
> won't we be stars, looking down from
> above,
> consumed.
> Yet here I stand, too afraid
> to complain—
> infinitely consumed.

• • •   • • •   • • •

Disposable, that's how I feel.
You drown in substances,
not for one instant wondering—
Vodka. Scotch. Bourbon. Cocaine. Ketamine—
whether any of it made you more
or less in love, or if you might
ignite something worse—
scar me so deeply
I no longer feel
safe, or loved, or even wish
for myself something else.

If you can't confront the demons
that tear you apart, relapse every day,
or every week, or maybe it is all one
endless relapse—
and still, do you see me?
The deceit? You can't free yourself, but
me? *I love you. I hate you. I love you.*
I can change.
This is me,
take it or leave it.

I never left your side—not until you'd
throw me away. Choose your
dealer over me. I dragged you to
Big Bear, praying nature could quiet the war.
I stayed through every spiral,
ate every name as you broke me, hacking away
at what little worth I had left. *Why are you even here?*
But I stayed every week, dragged you out of bed,
soothed and talked you out of it
again, and yet is it true you love
turmoil, are you so restless now
that for all my solace, all my support
so unwavering, you wake up guilty,
begging for an embrace—
can I love your addiction away? I did it
today, but what about tomorrow—
and what if love was never the cure?

I accept it all, love in its place.
My unspoken words echo
every night—flickers of hope,
despair's grip, an enduring flame
just within sight. Oh, what more can I do?
I lock myself out, but my sadness
forever stays.

Grieving the Living

I grieve a love still breathing—
a loss I never meant to meet,
a future that keeps hovering,
never landing,
one breath from breaking.

Every day carries the threat,
the way you gamble with your life
as if one more pull
won't decide it.

I leave unfinished,
each step rehearsing
what I could never save.

I gave you everything I had.
It was never enough.

Maybe I didn't love what was—
maybe I loved the shape
of what could be.

I let go not because I stopped loving you,
but because my spirit
couldn't survive the waiting.

Purgatory

You wake, and the world feels heavier—
as if the air remembers
every version of you
that tried to save him.

In dreams,
you still find him whole—
soft-eyed, unbroken,
a future you swore
was waiting for you.
There, you breathe freely.

But waking drags you back
to the shape of the truth—
a life spent as a passenger
to his own undoing,
promises thinned to threads,
love that evaporates
as quickly as he swears it.

You learn to live
inside the in-between—
the hours where night carries mercy
and morning carries the wound.

A place where memory and desire
refuse to let go,
where you stand suspended
between who he really was
and who you kept believing he could be.

This is purgatory—
the quiet punishment
of surviving a love
that never survived you.

Tear-Stained Face

Incessantly they fall,
as if I were swimming in them.

I don't know what I was addicted to—
you, or the repetition of you.

Consumed by you,
consuming substances—

You disappeared into powder and needles;
I stayed behind the looking glass.

I knelt in the wreckage,
mistaking it for faith.

Now sober in the aftermath,
I weep through the residue of a borrowed high.

A river of tears
mourns you, lost in a dream.

The sky still weeps,
but I've stopped counting the storms.

Orchestra of Silence

The pounding—
what's left of my heart—
echoes through these hours.
My bedroom hums too loud.
The wall,
the sun–
watched you vanish
while I remained.
My trembling body
folds, unfolds,
pleading to the ceiling,
someone above—
intervene.

Thoughts...
(a bag over my head)
Where are you?
Are you safe?

No glow. No pulse—
just the dark rectangle
waiting with me.

The clock-tick takes the room.

Absence
becomes my new heartbeat,
a hollow percussion,
an endless orchestra
etched into bone.

blood on my hands

What if my absence
could be the final dose—
the night your body decides
to stop trying.

I live on contingency.
Every goodbye rehearsed.
Every hour away—
a calculated risk.

Your family's name
engraved in my phone,
waiting for night
to confirm it.

How much of my life
have I spent
afraid my leaving would kill you.

Section III: The Reckoning

To see clearly,
we sit with the fog.
Here,
the war turns inward.

The Dialogue Within

My brain and heart, misaligned—
a dialogue well-defined.

> **Logic takes the floor:**
> *"We are moving on—*
> *we deserve more.*
> *You know this;*
> *you feel it in your core."*

Heart gently replies:
"He doesn't mean to hurt me.
He's trying.
It's the drugs that dim his light,
not the man I once held tight."

> **Brain interrupts:**
> *"Excuses.*
> *You're cut up, bruised—still here.*
> *When was the last time*
> *he checked in*
> *just because?"*

Heart:
"Brain, can you be still?
Your thoughts drown my will.
So intense and loud—
why are your thoughts even allowed?"

> **Brain again:**
> *"I'm the voice of reason—*
> *without me, it's treason.*
> *You're not even happy—*
> *just enduring.*
> *Tell me, Heart,*

Brain (cont.):
do you even love us,
or is suffering what you're idolizing?"

Heart:
"I love too much—
that's always been the problem.
He says he's done.
Sobriety has begun."

Brain:
"Another vow, another day—
he chose the needle, chose the K.
He blames the world, the stress, the sky...
but never once says sorry to you.
Why?"

Heart:
"You don't know him like I do.
I've given years—
he's drowning—
I'm his rope.
His only hope."

Brain:
"You're clinging to what if
instead of what is."

Heart:
"Maybe this time's different.
Maybe I caught him at the bottom."

Brain:
"He knows your threats are thin—
that's why you're still here."

Heart:
"I can't let go—
so I can't give you control."

> **Brain:**
> *"You never had control.*
> *Every stroke you take to stay afloat*
> *pulls you deeper in."*

Heart:
"Right now,
he says he loves me."

> **Brain (tired):**
> *"Because he knows you're almost free."*

Heart:
"I can help him—can't you see?"

> **Brain:**
> *"I disagree.*
> *He won't stay sober just for you.*
> *It won't last—*
> *your scars prove how this goes."*

Heart:
"If he overdoses?"

> **Brain:**
> *"That was never yours to stop."*

Heart:
"And what if he changes—
and someone else gets his peace
after I survived the nights?"

Brain:
"If 'what if' is how you measure love,
what does that say about your worth?"

Heart:
"I'll hold on a little longer,
maybe I'll get stronger."
(Maybe if I wait long enough,
I won't have to grieve.)

Brain:
"I love you, Heart, I really do—
but this isn't love.
It's a wound you choose."

Clockwork Heart

The mystery was never time,
but me—
my hunger for light
in borrowed hours.

Fireflies dazzled, gold through shadows.
I ran with a jar,
chasing their glow
like summer nights with you.

The hour hand slipped—
sober days flickered and fled,
fireflies rattling the jar,
never enough to hold.

I gave you my spare time.
Feeding the clock,
hands spinning faster,
fireflies leaking
through my cupped palms.

I inhaled your scent,
etched your laughter,
tried to bottle the glow
before it dimmed,
dreading the moment
the darkness claimed you back.

I lived in that light,
wanting to stay—
but time unlatched the jar
and the fireflies fled.

Now time jams—
a clockwork heart stalled.
I beg it to spin faster,
to erase even firefly light,
so night is only night—
and I can finally see you without the glow.

What's Left of Me

The air feels heavy.
My body sinks with it.
Breathing is work—
each inhale tight,
each thought
louder than the last.

I'm never here.
Lost in the past,
replaying what I should've said,
haunted by hours I gave
to someone who left.

Guilt gnaws
what's left of me.
Shame coats my skin—
all the lies I told
to cover you,
until I forgot
who I was without them.

Contorted

Bending, twisting,
shifting.
Abnormal—
yet habitual.

My spine
folded
and folded
into question marks.

Each vertebra,
a compromise.
Each breath,
a negotiation
with silence.

He called it love.
I called it
not
dying.

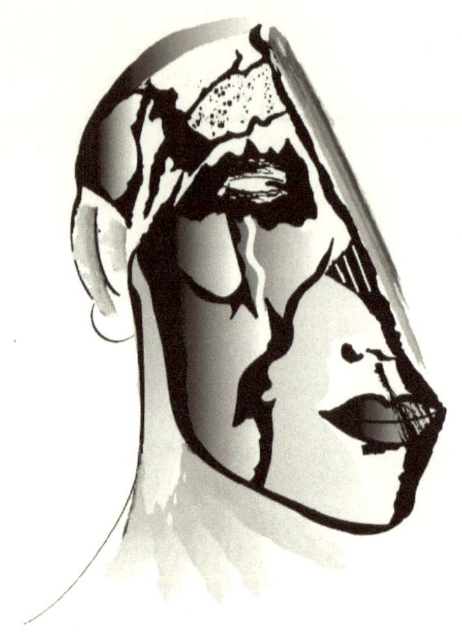

I Lost Me

I wanted to keep you close,
but self-erasure
tasted like love.

The more I reached in fear,
the more you became sand,
slipping
through clenched fists.

You used to press my smile,
between pages—
a keepsake.

Now I'm torn paper,
buried
beneath your latest lies.

Meals became memory.
I wilted without touch.
Hours slipped without sound.

My skin no longer fit—
I ached
and everything blurred
into nothing.

No music.
Just your smile,
twirling me in circles
like the ending was real.

I dreamt of vows.
A white dress.
Your grin
waiting at the aisle.

Now absence sings instead.
My spirit, once fire,
burned itself out
to keep you warm.

111
Hopes & Dreams
4:44

The Train Platform

Alpine wind cuts cold
along the platform
where strangers disembark,
eyes full of other lives.

I clutch my golden ticket,
my name etched deep.
This is the one I've waited for
since I first learned
the cost
of waking from a dream.

The wait feels long.
But I stay—
nerves shaking,
steadied by belief.

Beside me, a stranger lingers,
your eyes—familiar,
like a life I once lived
and ache to relive.

There's warmth in you,
the kind I only recognize
from books I underlined,
hoping it was real.

We laugh.
Time disappears.

For a moment, I wonder
if the ticket was never mine to keep.

You mention popcorn—
but I feel it:
the train approaching.
Your kiss—
my lips
soft on yours.

You promise to follow.
Tell me not to cry.
You step away.

Deep down,
I know.

The whistle screams.
The platform shakes.
The ground says choose.

"All aboard,"
 the conductor calls.

I hesitate.

You're still behind—
tethered by fear,
wounds
you won't name.

I almost stay.
God,
I almost do.

But my ticket pulses in my palm—
the journey
etched at birth.

The doors close.
The train exhales.
I press my hand to the glass.
Your figure blurs.

I know.
You won't run.
You never did.

The train moves on.

My heart breaks.
Something else opens.

The train whispers
what I've known all along:
I was meant to board—
meant to find you,
never meant to keep you.

After the Magic

Every bone still aches for the dream—
the love spell I mistook
for fate.
It didn't end in fire.
The candles didn't burn.
I didn't notice the cold
until I did.

One night,
the words stopped working.
Your promises
lost their heat.
You chose your path.
I chose mine.
The spell didn't shatter.
It wore off.
We stopped believing.

The White Wall

How many shades of color
can a white wall wear?

In the morning, it blushes orange.
What will it wear today?
A melody floods my mind,
loops through silence.
Down the bridge of my nose,
salt on my lips.
Drip.
Drip.
Drip.

How many shades of color
can a white wall wear?

Afternoon.
The sun is there—
but it's missing.
Light, but not warmth.
The shadows grow longer,
like fingers crawling toward me.

My body
is here.
I think.

The phone buzzes—
(unnoticed.)

A crack in the corner of the ceiling—
new, maybe.
Or has it always been there?

A speck of dust dances in a sunbeam.
It matters.
It doesn't.
It matters.
I don't.

How many shades of color
can a white wall wear?

I inhale.
Or try to.
You have clogged
my nose, chest, bones.

The sunset never mirrors the sunrise.
What began in hope
ends in grief.
The sound escapes—
the one I've been holding
for hours, days.
A splintering pain in my chest.
Like a star that's run out of fuel.
Collapsing inward,
until only dust.

How many shades of color
can a white wall wear?

How many shades of color
can a white wall wear
before I disappear with it?

The Snow Globe

I watch from my perch on the mantle—
serenity sealed in glass,
a world apart from the room's hum,
watching love burn bright, then dim.

The couple curled like Velcro—
two as one, disappearing into night.

But slowly, cracks appeared—
not in the globe, but in them.
Arguments lit the air,
distress flares over dark water.

I heard everything they loved
fade into static.

He turned to the bottle—
she bent, then broke, then bent again.
He grew deaf to pleas,
blind to ruin.

A suitcase waited by the door.
Tears salted the wood floor.
She left—
to salvage—well, something.

Guilt coiled at his throat.
He dug deeper into numbness,
avoiding mirrors,
erasing memories—
until he couldn't escape me anymore.
His hands met my glass in violent flight.

I shattered.
Fake snow swirled
in a blizzard of regret.
Liquid bled through floorboards—
their tiny world dissolved.

When morning came,
I lay in shards,
reflecting what remained—
love so sharp
no hand dared touch it.

Collateral

No one talks
about the collateral damage—
the ones who love the addict.

I stayed because I was tethered—
addicted to your love,
weak with fear
of what leaving would do.

Because I didn't want you to die.

Those nights—
pacing the floor,
phone in one hand,
your suicide letter in the other—
hoping this time
it was only a threat.

I held your secrets,
swallowed your shame,
carried your guilt
so you wouldn't
carry it to your grave.

You said if you overdosed,
your blood would be on my hands
for walking away.
I believed you.
For years, I did.

I thought love was a lifeline—
that letting go
was the cut.

But the truth was quieter:
I mistook rescue for love,
devotion for survival.

You passed me the weight
you couldn't bear,
called it care—
and I wore it.

I still mourn
the five years
I gave to the fire.
My twenties—
a war diary
with love notes in the margins.

I thought I was saving you.
I was just burning slower.

Echoes on the Wooden Dock

On the wooden dock, I tread.
Each plank creaks beneath me—
reminders of choices made,
paths I can't retrace.

Splinters find my feet—
tiny doubts lodged deep.

Behind me,
the forest hums—
familiar, dangerous,
a lullaby of ruin.

Ahead, the lake—
a black mirror,
moonless, waiting.

I pause.
The wind still howls,
though the sky is clear.

A whisper stirs within—
the voice I've tried to silence.
It tells me: jump.

But the forest calls as well—
its pull almost tender,
whispering my name.

One tear
for what I mistook for shelter.

Toes grip the edge—
I offer fear my hand,
and leap.
The water closes around me—
cold, clean,
strangely quiet.

Between What Was & What's Next

Dear Reader,

If you've made it to this point in the journey, let's pause together. Let's stand on this dock between what was and what comes next.

Healing isn't linear. It doesn't follow a perfect arc; it twists, doubles back, stumbles forward, and sometimes leaves you standing still. Some days you'll feel strong. Other days you'll ache for what you let go—even when you know it hurt you, even when you were pulled into their chaos—loving them the way survival teaches you to.

If you see yourself in these pages—in the clinging, the hope, the heartbreak, the desperate bargains—please know this: you are not weak. You are not foolish. You are human.

You don't have to hate yourself to walk away. You don't need to stop loving them to choose yourself. Every stage of this journey was necessary—the parts where I stayed too long, the moments I lost myself, the nights I whispered their name and wished for one more chance.

What comes next isn't the end of the heartbreak. It is the beginning of reclaiming what I lost—myself.

Leaving what hurts us doesn't erase the love we felt, or the guilt, or the pull to look back. Wherever you are in your own story, be gentle with yourself. You are not broken. You are not alone. You are allowed to forgive yourself for the messy, gut-wrenching feelings that come with doing the right thing.

Let's take a breath here. The dock is solid beneath us. The current hums with what's next. And when you're ready, we'll step into the unknown together.

With love,
Annie Hopex

Section IV: The Turning

You don't rise in one great moment.
You rise quietly,
with decisions no one sees but
you.

The Anchor of Reality pt. II

Alone.
Thrashing.
Salt fills my mouth.
The sea crushes my lungs.

You left,
but your chaos stayed—
a weight around my ankles,
pulling me under
while you reach for another buoy.

I was used, discarded:
mere driftwood.

Abandoned,
the night swallows me whole.

The abyss became all I knew.
Its current spun grief and guilt—
up, down—no difference.
I drowned.

A gull cries—
sharp, far—
proof the world above still exists.

Beyond the dark,
light waits.

Chains bite,
but clarity cuts deeper.
My bone-weary ankles throb.
Calves seize.
I thrash.

I claw at the barnacled chain.
Hands withered and pruned,
burning, blistering.

One ankle slips free.

Do I want this?
What if you return—
to save me,
as I once saved you?

Above, a smear of
burnt orange—
mornings I had forgotten.

The other ankle shakes free.
Weightless, I rise,
buoyed by what was mine all along.

Below, the whirlpool spins.
Dark but beautiful—
the way your eyes once were:
tender, but built to drown me.
Luring. Hungry. Lethal.

I turn toward the light.

Breaking through—
air, sharp and clean.
Lashes dripping,
salt burning my eyes.

Waves still batter me.
The sea does not forgive.
I float while choking—
not happiness,
but finally breathing.

After the Fire

I always asked
what you needed—
water? sleep? forgiveness?

Should I stay?
I never asked—
what do *I* want?

Maybe peace.
Stillness that doesn't beg,
love that doesn't make me wait.

A room where I can cry
without apology
for taking up space.

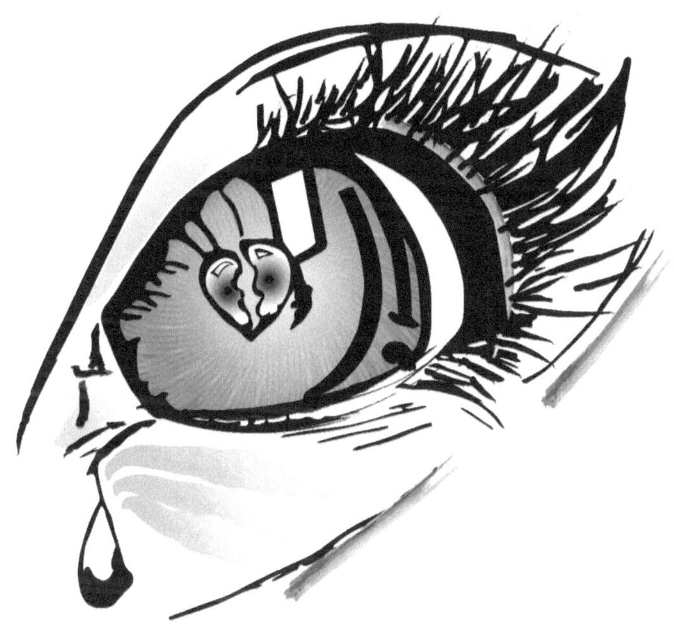

Blue Eyes

My blue eyes
once bright,
bleached pale by tears—
now shadows pool
where light lived.

Ocean blue—
diluted.
The tide pulls back,
steals sea-glitter with it—
salt remains.

A blue jay flashes past—
rare as forgiveness—
its song thin as
broken glass.

Blueberries—
sweet in June—
collapse, bitter
on my tongue.

Forget-me-nots—
our magical flower.
Our season ended.
Petals curl into dust.

A shade of blue lost
with my heart.
I wear what remains,
learning the slow act
of how to restart.

Past Lives

We built fires
in caves,
palaces in Egypt,
tenements in France—
each time believing
we could keep the light.

In every age,
the ending found us early:
a sword, a fever, a sea—
always something claiming you first.

And now—
this life,
this body,
this heart,
this addiction.
The same lesson returned,
disguised by a different name.

I swear our souls bargained
before they fell—
their echoes still hum
beneath the silence,
our names carved
where the scars remember us.

You reached for the flame,
and I lingered too long
in its glow.

Still, across lifetimes,
I feel your leaving—
not as doom,
but something that always comes.

We'll meet again,
when the cycle is broken,
when the fire is out,
and all that remains
is love that no longer saves,
but simply *is*.

House of Decay

When I was young,
dreams of gold—
love spun from longings:
princes and promises,
houses built with laughter
that never broke,
foundations poured from love.

But bulbs flickered.
The paint peeled.
The walls began to whisper.
The roof wept;
the house grew tired.

Still, I thought if I worked harder,
the walls might hold.

I patch the floor beams again,
hammering until my hands ache—
not to rebuild,
but because I can't stand
stepping on the nails.

I beg the foundation to remember,
but it keeps slipping
through my hands.

Eventually, the nails felt safer
than starting over.
I learn to lie still
with sharp things beneath me—
at least that pain is predictable.

It's 3 A.M.,
and you're nowhere to be found.
Was it a leak that woke me,
or fear from before?
You promised—
you were done.

Then—the familiar sound:
fumbling.
Cabinets clatter.
I follow.

The floors crack and scream
with every step,
begging me to not see
what I already know.

One hand on the knob,
I stand in the doorway—
heart hammering
like the pipes
that never stop groaning.

You're slumped over
on the bathroom floor.
Empty needles in the sink.

You swear you'll fix it tomorrow—
the leak, the mess, yourself.
But tomorrow never moves in.

I box up memories
through heavy air,
label them carefully:

Fall in Rhode Island.
Thanksgiving in San Diego.
Solvang Christmas.
Dust and mold claimed all of them—
except one:
the part of me
that refused to rot.

Through tears,
I whisper goodbye
to walls that held us,
to ceilings too low
for who I've become,
to pillows that caught
every tear that fell.

The foundation is gone.
The bond, a ghost.
And this house—this love—
no longer holds me.

GUARANTEED
PAIN
OLD PICTURES
FISHING FOR ANXIETY
STALKING SOCIAL MEDIA
MEMORY LANE
REREADING TEXTS
SALE

Pain Shopping

I try to resist,
but curiosity's lethal lure
pulls me under—
cracks
slip through.

I scroll through shadows:
new followers, tagged photos,
grainy glimpses I shouldn't see.
My pulse hammers with each clue
I never needed.

I stitch the story myself—
scraps becoming scenes,
imagined laughter,
worlds you built without me.

Still, I chase it,
I know the drop will follow—
my chest hollow,
and yet I keep digging.

Why feed this hunger,
when it only eats me?
Why keep reopening the wound
when I'm the one who bleeds?

Nothing here is happening
to me.
I'm doing it.

The Pinecone

In the hush before dawn,
a pinecone loosens its hold—
not an ending,
but a shedding.

It falls onto untouched snow,
its weight barely a whisper,
yet the earth beneath it remembers
what patience is for.

I don't see it,
buried in white,
until my body learns
the ground won't move with me.

The fall is abrupt.
The silence louder than the impact.
Some stops are not gentle—
they are deliberate.

The forest doesn't react.
It never does.
It knows interruption
is part of the arrangement.

Somewhere above,
the wind carries a name
I won't understand yet—
only that forward
is no longer an option.

Time slows into stillness.
Healing becomes something I can't rush.
That's when the truth arrives—
not loud,
not cruel,
just undeniable.

The pinecone dreams of roots and fire,
of waiting out the cold.
Closed tight, it can't become anything.
It knows falling isn't failure—
only when it stops reaching upward
can it begin to grow inward.

Mine was heavy with hope,
polished smooth by repetition.
When it dropped, it didn't shatter.
It made staying impossible.

I didn't fall to be broken.
I fell so the forest
could finally take root
where he wasn't.

The Last Box

I'm not sure this is the end.
But I know I can't stay—
waiting for a version of you
that may never come.

It's not your flaws—
I could love those.
When the dark days held you under,
sleeping through the hours,
I could love that—
even the spirals,
the nights you stayed up chasing dreams
that burned out by dawn.

But it's your refusal to change,
to meet me in the fire
with watered eyes and trembling hands
instead of gasoline and promises.

I kept rewriting our story—
made myself the caretaker,
the calm in your chaos,
the one who filled every crack with hope.
But I was only patching
damage your silence kept alive,
pretending stillness meant safety.

I said I'd never leave.
And for a long time, I didn't.
I stayed through a thousand small endings—
forgotten baggies tucked into drawers,
emails of apologies,
your knock on my window at 5 A.M.,
the lies that softened just enough to believe,

mornings you swore
this time would be different.
I broke
a little more each time
before I finally
opened the door.

There were good days.
You'd scramble eggs, burn the bagels,
kiss my forehead,
wrap your arms around me,
say, *this is forever*.

Sometimes it felt like we shared one mind—
finishing each other's sentences.
And then the nights when your laugh,
our laugh,
left my ribs aching,
tears of joy salt-bright on my cheeks.
Falling asleep to your hand in my hair,
your voice a low promise:
I'll never lose you again.

And still—
you chose the bottle,
your dealer,
the powder,
the high, the lies.

I learned to make your silence sound like peace,
to pretend the signs weren't there—
to blame it on a bad day,
a bad week,
a bad month.

But I'm here now—
not angry,
not bitter,
just tired.

The last box is in my hands.
Labeled *miscellaneous*,
but I know what's inside:
a Valentine's card—
your promise never to lose me,
torn in half
in front of my face.
Photobooth pictures of us in love,
the apology I never received
and finally stopped begging for.

This is not revenge.
Not punishment.
Only love—
given
to the one who needed it most:
me.

Letter of Forgiveness

I'm sorry
for how often
I left you behind—
for making your needs
the last on the list,
then never getting to you at all.

And for every time I said,
hold on a little longer,
when you were already falling—
in every way a person can.

I didn't notice the storm—
or maybe I did, and looked away—
until I was
stumbling in the dark.

To my heart—
I'm sorry.

Summer Meets Winter

Summer, the season that held its ground—
salt-bright skin, the sea's low sound.
Jasmine thick, the days unbroken,
nothing aching, nothing hidden.

Winter, the season of frost and hush—
skies draped in a crystalline blush.
Woodsmoke curls through evergreen halls,
a world held still as soft snow falls.

Spring

Spring came hard and fast between us.
Touch felt necessary.
Love felt urgent,
we burned toward each other
like relief was proof,
like intensity meant forever.

For my warm touch,
the ice around his heart broke.

Autumn

Autumn arrived before anything shattered.
The days grew shorter. He pulled inward.
I reached for his light
but met shadows instead.

I couldn't name what was wrong—
and that was how I knew.

Winter

Winter closed in.
Whatever warmth remained turned to frost.
I knocked and pleaded,
but the season wouldn't change.

ANNIE HOPE

When Goodbye is Love

Sometimes I wish you were a bad person.
It would have made leaving easy.

A knife that doesn't pierce—
just drags and drags.

I loved you
where you couldn't stay.

So I walked away—
not to punish you,
but to survive myself.

Letting Go

The hardest heartbreak I have known
is learning how to leave you alone.

The cruelest heartbeat bangs—
I thought I might die
before learning restraint.
I bargained,
without knowing why.

One night, I sat on the beach,
asked the Lady Moon,
said goodbye out loud.
Nothing answered—
only my own voice
crashing back to me.

Perhaps I always knew
the places I called home
were never permanent.
I lived on possibility.
I ignored what was.

When I finally stopped reaching
I wasn't relieved.
A stranger
stared back at me.

The silence didn't open into peace.
It filled with arguments—
part of me choosing reality,
the other refusing to wake.

There was nothing to do
but wipe my face
after I cried.

And cried again.
Grief didn't vanish—
it thinned.
And in that thinning,
I saw how much of myself
I had lost trying to stay.

Leaving you wasn't the ending.
It was the moment
I stopped disappearing.

Section V: The Becoming

Not healed.
But whole.
Stronger not because it hurt—but because
you faced it and
kept going.

ANNIE HOPE

Weights I Wear

There's a weight I've learned to bear—
not heavy enough to break,
but deep enough to ache.
It settles like rain in quiet air,
a muted echo, dense enough to notice.

At first, it cut—
not clean,
more like glass in the heel,
every step reminding me
I was still walking.

Now it hums.
Or maybe that's my blood.
Or the fridge at midnight.
Or nothing.

I don't outrun it.
I don't push it away.
I let it walk beside me.

Its shadow—
not sharp,
not cruel—
something I know by shape.

It lives in the unguarded hours.
An undergarment,
invisible to strangers.

The weight is still here.
It doesn't ask my permission.
But it no longer keeps me
from setting things down.

Breaking the Chain

A poor little stranger,
eyes open,
filled with eager potential,
chasing futures
that never arrived.

Dragged by her own shadow,
puppeteered
into motion.

Days folded into years—
roundabouts.
Dead ends.
She learned the shape of waiting
without knowing she could stop.

One day,
she did.

Not gracefully—
hesitation in her steps,
hands unsure what to do
when no one pulled the strings.

She moved forward anyway.
Slow.
Unsteady.
The kind of progress
that doesn't feel like victory.

She pauses.
Breathes.
Hears the chain fall.

She isn't a poor little stranger anymore.
She doesn't run.

She walks,
choosing the ground
one step at a time.

Metamorphosis

An egg hatches on a leaf,
eyes open to a world anew.
A slinky caterpillar sighs in relief,
nestled in morning dew.

It munches everything green,
growing, doubling in size—
shedding its skin unseen,
beneath forgiving skies.

But soon its body slows,
its skin begins to harden—
as if its form just froze,
fearing death within the garden.

It hides beneath the branches,
seeking solitude to die.
Longing for the days it danced,
it whispers one last goodbye.

It forms a silken tomb,
inside, everything unravels—
muscle, memory, identity—
a soft and silent undoing.

Dying, disintegrating,
alone inside the dark—
only a hum of endings
and the ache of becoming.

It dissolves into soup.
Tissues, limbs, organs shift.
The shape forgets what it was
to remember what comes next.

Cocoon

All it took was one life ending
for another to become comfortable—
for now.
I like it here.
It's safe.

That surprises me.
I once prayed for this stillness.

The walls around me
draw closer each day.
They hum
as I rock back and forth—

not an ending,
just containment.

Something in me
keeps tracing the edges.
Not because I want to leave,
but because I could.

I don't rush.
Wings need time
to remember
how to hold themselves.

Liminal

The cocoon hasn't changed.
I have.
The stillness did its work.
Now it presses back.

The wings have found
their heartbeat—
soft,
natural.

They move in small ways.
Practicing.
Waiting for
what opens next.

Flight of Surrender

Nothing but elsewhere in the flight.
No ground.
No instrument that stays where I put it.

I steer anyway—
tilt the sky,
call it control.

Calm, and then suddenly not.
Warnings blare.
The storm, the lightning, the wind—
or perhaps it's not.
Maybe it is only this grip,
the belief
that everything depends on me.

I grip.
I release.
I grip—
my hands refusing
what my mind already knows.

The nose dips low,
my hands reach
before I can stop them.

I try to hold the altitude.
Try to keep us level.
As if I were meant
to fly more than one life.

Then something gives.
Not the plane—
my hands.

I am not the pilot.
I never was.

I am a passenger in the sky.

And suddenly,
the weight I was carrying
has a place to go.

The flight continues.
So does the turbulence.
But now,
what's mine to carry
is enough.

Gold

I gave the love back
not because it was wrong—
but because it wasn't yours to hold
forever.

Today's Promise

Just for today,
I will love myself fully—
put my feelings first,
guard the heart that kept me alive.

Today,
I will choose what's uncomfortable
if it leads somewhere honest—
trusting my steps matter.

In this moment,
I will welcome my old feelings—
listen without judgment,
then let them go.

In this day,
I turn toward the light—
not because shadows are gone,
but because I know where I'm standing.

This breath,
I welcome more than I expected—
morning, wind, the quiet joy
of being here.

Only today
I make these promises,
to stay present,
and to treat myself with care.

This is enough
for now.

A Gift to Myself

I never would have chosen this path.
Still—there is proof here
of how deeply I can love.

It hurt because it was real.
And letting go did not erase it.

I am learning what is mine—
my time,
my body,
the quiet voice that knows when to stop.

Some things are not for me to carry.
Some things are.
Some days I remember.
Some days I forget.

Just for today
I place the love back
where it can't hurt
me.

That is the work.
That is the gift.

A Note of Leaving

Dear Reader,

If you're here now, thank you—for reading, for feeling, for staying.

This book doesn't end in resolution, because neither does healing. I haven't made it to the other side. But I continue to show up for myself, even on the days it doesn't feel like enough.

Some days still ache. Some memories still sting. But now I know how to hold space for both the pain and the progress. That is the quiet victory.

If you're holding grief, heartbreak, or the weight of loving someone who's still lost—know that you're not alone. You're allowed to choose yourself. You're allowed to rest. You're allowed to be whole, even with scars.

Keep going.
Keep choosing you.

The anchor is within you now.

With love and deep respect,
Annie Hope